MW00613783

Setting the Table

Setting the Table

Poems by LINDA PASTAN
with illustrations by Mark Leithauser

Dryad Press
WASHINGTON, D.C. & SAN FRANCISCO

Printed in the United States of America.

Some of these poems have appeared in the following periodicals: *The American Magazine, Bits, Choice, Field, The Long Pond Review, The Massachusetts Review, The Nation, Poetry, Southern Voices, Tinderbox.*

"Snow" first appeared in Wang Hui-Ming, *The Land on the Tip of a Hair* (Barre Publishers, 1972).

"Butter," "Popcorn," and "A Symposium: Apples" appeared in *Aspects of Eve*, poems by Linda Pastan. Copyright © 1970, 1971, 1972, 1974, 1975 by Linda Pastan. "Egg" and "Soup" appeared in *The Five Stages of Grief*, poems by Linda Pastan. Copyright © 1978 by Linda Pastan. Selections reprinted with the permission of the publisher, W. W. Norton and Company, Inc., New York, N. Y., and the author.

Library of Congress
Cataloging in Publication data:
Pastan, Linda, 1932–
Setting the table.
I. Title.
PS3566.A775S4 811'.5'4 79-15833
ISBN 0-931848-26-1
ISBN 0-931848-25-3 lim. ed.

This publication was supported by a grant from the National Endowment for the Arts in Washington, D.C., a federal agency.

DRYAD PRESS
P. O. Box 1656, Washington, D.C. 20013.
P. O. Box 29161, Presidio,
San Francisco, California 94129.

For Myra

CONTENTS

SETTING THE TABLE

The lemon
is no heavier
than its own shadow
in this late afternoon
light. It is time
to cover the table
with the cloth, to spread
the white cloth
and watch it settle
as a bird settles its wings
over the nest
after a long
flight.

I set three places,
noticing the places
I no longer set.
I arrange a still life:
napkin fork knife
and one spoon shaped
to the mouth
of the last child,
and one to the mouth
of the old woman
whose surprised face
rises
out of mine.

I believed the promise
of the lemon in bud,
and though the fruit is bitter
I will share it with you
against the time
when silver
chimes
against china,
when upon the plate's round face
one of us rests his fork
and knife for the last time—
the two stilled hands
of a clock.

PETIT DEJEUNER

I sing a song
of the croissant
and of the wily French
who trick themselves daily
back to the world
for its sweet ceremony.
Ah to be reeled
up into morning
on that crisp,
buttery
hook.

BUTTER

You held the butter-
cup under my chin
and laughed: "get thee
to a buttery,"
chewing on a dandelion stem,
then tasting my
buttery fingers
one by one
and eyeing
my breasts as if
they too could,
bobbing, churn
pure milk to
butter.
Yellow dress and
flowers, yellow
hair, the world
was melting butter
sweet and slick,
your hands all yellow
with the spilling
sun, desire
like the heated
knife through
butter.

EGG

In this kingdom
the sun never sets;
under the pale oval
of the sky
there seems no way in
or out,
and though there is a sea here
there is no tide.

For the egg itself
is a moon
glowing faintly
in the galaxy of the barn,
safe but for the spoon's
ominous thunder,
the first delicate crack
of lightning.

AUBADE

In the early morning
I shake my head
to clear away the static
of the dream
the way my daughter
shakes the radio she holds
against her ear
as if it were a shell.
On the table between us
the sun spreads
its slow stain;
fog lifts
from the coffee;
a heart drifts out of reach
on the surface
of the milk.
Now my daughter takes the day
into her hand
like fresh baked bread—
she offers me a piece.

SNOW

Snow seeks its own level,
falling into barrels,
over curbstones, up to
the branching of trees.
I have seen crystals of salt
fall out of solution
with the same single
gesture and cold white milk
poured as deliberately
from bottle to glass.

SOUP

"A rich man's soup—and all from a few stones."
Marcia Brown, *Stone Soup*

If your heart feels
like a stone
make stone soup of it.
Borrow the parsley
from a younger woman's garden.
Dig up a bunch of phallic carrots.
Your own icebox is full
of the homelier vegetables.
Now cry into the pot.
When he comes home
serve him a steaming bowlful.
Then watch him as he bites
into the stone.

BARBECUE

In the late light
of Indian summer
we stand
with our burnt
offerings,
watching the sky
become charred with evening
lost in the smell
of the meat
as we remember
each in his own flesh
the old weather
of the hunt.

FORTUNE COOKIES

These pursed lips say:
"somewhere an old lover
still thinks of you"
"fortune lies in a
westerly direction"
"beware of travel."
All this will come true,
is true already, folded
into the dough like a hankie
into a stranger's pocket,
or a ship magically
bottled in glass
on which we must all sail.

I have watched women beat
the eggs with a secret
turn of the wrist,
have seen them measure
the sugar, the salt,
the almond whose song
Li Po recognized.
Children break the cookies
with the crisp sound
of a latch on a door
they dare to open: "the young
think the old are fools,
the old know the young are."

CHOCOLATES

Plump,
swaddled in silver
or gold,
rows of them
each in its tiny cradle
waiting to be picked
first, tempting us
with glossy faces
to the fifth
deadly sin.

And we succumb,
remembering the briberies
of childhood
when we passed them
in bars like gold
over the counter.
Now we sink sweetly,
achingly in,
up to the
hilt.

POPCORN

When Plato said
that what we see are shadows
flickering on a cave wall,
he must have meant
the movies.
You let a cigarette lean
from your mouth precisely
as Bogart did.
Because of this, reels later
we say of our life
that it is B grade;
that it opened and will close
in a dusty place where
things move always
in slow motion;
that what is real
is the popcorn
jammed between our teeth.

A SYMPOSIUM: APPLES

Eve Remember a season
of apples, the orchard
full of them, my apron
full of them. One day
we wandered from tree
to tree, sharing a basket
feeling the weight of apples
increase between us.
And how your muscles ripened
with all that lifting.
I felt them round and hard
under my teeth; white
and sweet the flesh
of men and apples.

Gabriel Nameless in Eden,
the apple itself
was innocent—an ordinary
lunchpail fruit.
Still it reddened
for the way it was used.
Afterward the apple
chose for itself
names untrusting
on the tongue: stayman
gravenstein,
northern spy.

The Serpent Ordinary, innocent
yes. But deep
in each center of whiteness
one dark star...

Adam In the icebox
an apple
will keep
for weeks.
Then its skin
wrinkles up
like the skin of the old man
I have become,
from a single
bite.

PRUNUS MUME

for Joan and Peter

You chose from the Japanese
a plum tree whose delicate
calligraphy scents parchments,
haiku, soup bowls, documents
of courtship. It gives you
instead of dusky night plums,
high noon apricots. How strange,
as when the goose saw in all
that barny straw not the
usual plain egg but one
of gold; or, walking between
white columns into a house
of federal grey, to be
greeted not with cool welcome
but with a scramble of dogs
and children.

PEARS

Some say
it was a pear
Eve ate.
Why else the shape
of the womb,
or of the cello
whose single song is grief
for the parent tree?
Why else the fruit itself
tawny and sweet
which your lover
over breakfast
lets go your pear-
shaped breast
to reach for?

HOME FOR THANKSGIVING

The gathering family
throws shadows around us,
it is the late afternoon
of the family.

There is still enough light
to see all the way back,
but at the windows
that light is wasting away.

Soon we will be nothing
but silhouettes: the sons'
as harsh
as the fathers'.

Soon the daughters
will take off their aprons
as trees take off their leaves
for winter.

Let us eat quickly—
let us fill ourselves up.
The covers of the album are closing
behind us.

THE LAST FOOD POEM

Let this be
the last food poem.
We have learned civics
from the salad
where all lettuces are equal;
fealty from the butter
cleaving to its bread.
It is time to sit
at a real table and eat,
whispering for grace
one final couplet:
raspberries
and cream.

Setting the Table was designed and composed
in ATF Bulmer types by Roland A. Hoover.
This edition was prepared from photographically
reduced reproduction proofs of the original
letterpress edition (250 signed and numbered
copies). One thousand copies have been printed
by offset lithography on 80-lb Mohawk Superfine
Text by Paul Trimble at The Writer's Center,
Glen Echo, Maryland, and bound by Perfect
Books, Inc., Baltimore, Maryland.